Understanding the Five-Fold Ministry

Don and Sharon Duke

authorHOUSE

AuthorHouse™
1663 Liberty Drive
Bloomington, IN 47403
www.authorhouse.com
Phone: 1-800-839-8640

First published by AuthorHouse 5/9/2011

ISBN: 978-1-4520-8253-0 (sc)

Library of Congress Control Number: 2011903010

Printed in the United States of America

This book is printed on acid-free paper.

CONTENTS

THE DEFINITION OF UNDERSTANDING

"When I say that I shall use the foolish to confound the wise, then it shall be as I have written, and those who try to understand those things in the natural will truly be confused; as they will continue to be blind to those things in the heavenlies and those things which are to be in the future.

" Know this, that the word, <u>under</u>, means to be beneath and to be overwhelmed by something that is over, or on top, or greater than what you can ever imagine in all of your wildest dreams.

"The word, <u>stand</u>, on the other hand, is to be firm, or to be straight or upright in a position, where you know that you are in a place where you must be, that you were ordained to be at this particular time in your life.

"When you put these two words together and the meanings they both have separate from one another, then you have the word, <u>understand</u>, which means to be beneath a position of righteousness with the one who created you from the very beginning - to know that you know who you are under this position of where you have been placed for a particular point and time in your life.

"People who say they understand do not know what they are saying many times, because they are not under the position of righteousness of God, their Creator, Author, Savior, Deliverer, and the one who they will spend eternity with all of the days of their lives."

We all need to be beneath the position of righteousness with our Heavenly Father and be in that secret hiding place where the angels and the brush of angels' wings surround us all of those times when we are not even aware they are there, because we are only able to see with limited natural vision in the physical and not with supernatural vision in the spiritual realm.

FOREWORD

After Don received individual ministry at the Checotah Revival in Checotah, Oklahoma on February 27, 2000, the Holy Spirit began pouring out thoughts, words, and teachings for him to write down, up to ten pages a day in the beginning. These teachings and instructions have continued every day since that time.

The first book, A Journey with the Father, was published from those writings in the year 2008, intending to equip believers for the return of Jesus Christ and the last days of the Latter Rain of God's great and final outpouring of His Spirit.

Don and Sharon's visit to the revival in February 2000, completely changed the direction of their lives, and they went back many times. God called them to leave the corporate world behind for something much greater.

Rainbow Jubilee Ministry was birthed on Easter Sunday, 2000. All quotations, if not designated as taken from the King James Bible, are taken from these writings. Website: www.rainbowjubileeinc. com

The following scriptures helped them understand how these writings are so powerful, yet precious, not only in their own daily lives, but are intended to give hope, strength, and courage to those who have eyes to see and ears to hear:

I Chronicles 28:19: All this, said David, the Lord made me understand in writing by his hand upon me, even all the works of this pattern. (KJV)

Psalm 45:1: My heart is indicting a good matter; I speak of the things which I have made touching the king: My tongue is the pen of a ready writer. (KJV)

Jeremiah 36:1-2: And it came to pass in the fourth year of Jehojakim the son of Josiah King of Judah, that this word came unto Jeremiah from the Lord, saying, Take thee a roll of a book, and write therein all the words that I have spoken unto thee against Israel, and against Judah, and against all the nations, from the day I spake unto thee, from the days of Josiah, even unto this day. (KJV)

Revelation 14:13: And I (John) heard a voice from heaven saying unto me, 'Write: Blessed are the dead who die in the Lord from now on.' 'Yea", saith the Spirit, 'that they may rest from their labors; and their works do follow them.' (KJV)

Revelation 21:5: And he that sat upon the throne said, Behold, I make all things new. And he said unto me, Write: for these words are true and faithful. (KJV)

ACKNOWLEDGEMENTS

First and foremost, we acknowledge the wonderful Holy Spirit, who has led us to this place in our lives.

We extend heartfelt thanks to the following people:

To our parents, whose words live inside us, always.

Adult children - Kevin Ribnick, Mindy Esco, Jason Duke, and Amber Duke.

Our sisters and brothers, whose words made great impressions on us.

To all those friends along the way, whose lives touched and influenced ours.

To the churches we traveled through and learned from

THE PARADE OF SIN

"People do not say the truth about themselves, when you ask them how they are, or what is happening in their lives. You will need to know how to discern when they are telling you something they believe you want to hear from the truth. The truth will always be the last thing you will hear from My people, and it will come after the crust has been broken or removed from their wounded souls. My people's souls have been wounded by so many hurts over many misunderstood relationships, which have ended.

"People are hungry to have a relationship with each other but are unable to have a meaningful one, because of fear and pride. These two elements are the basic root cause why My people have not been able to be free.

"The demonic spirits of fear and pride are so strong that they can capture other demons, such as shyness, timidity, haughtiness, busyness, deceitfulness, and manipulation. There are others who will possess more cunning ways to divert you from their path; and they will send you to someone else, so you will not bother them.

"People are not aware that these spirits are dwelling inside their soul area and will tell you that everything is alright within their heart, because they do not know about their heart. People believe their heart is their soul. The heart is the window to their soul. When people say they have opened up their heart to you, or Jesus, they are saying that they see something through the window of their heart; but there is no way for you to get into their heart.

"The door to a person's soul is through the tongue of that person, when they speak life or death into the soul area. Sin is like a parade, marching around My people twenty-four hours a day, with many attractive displays of enticing thoughts and ideas to enter into their eyes and ears. My people have two of each, two eyes and two ears, to receive all of the attractive enticing displays put before their eyes and ears.

"When My people begin to focus on a particular display of sin in the twenty-four hour continuous parade, that sin will leave the parade and come to My people. The sin will begin to give them their own private showing of how much fun they are missing and how that person has longed for that particular sin.

"My people have not guarded their heart, which is the window of their soul. Their two eyes and two ears will dance around this sin, which has stopped to give My people their own private show. The eyes and ears will transfer the parade into their mind, so they cannot lose what the sin is all about. The mind will then begin to create more fun and exciting ways to have more fun with a particular sin.

"My people may keep this sin many months or years, but the parade has not stopped. The eyes and ears are still watching and calling for more private displays of sin to come into their minds and join in with the previous sins into the theater of My people's minds.

"They will then begin to create their own production within their own minds, because I have made My people to be creative. Soon they will have to seek other people who have created similar shows in the theater of their minds, so they can speak about itto each other and exchange ideas with one another how their production of sin can be improved to have more fun to feed the flesh of My hungry people.

"Once My people have begun to speak these things, the door to their soul will open and receive, with a flowing of rivers of water and cause a flood in their soul, washing out the purity and innocent seed, which I planted, while they were in their mother's womb. The soul has been flooded; My seed has been washed away by the flood; and My people have no seed to grow and produce fruit, for their souls have been washed away, as well, by the floodgates of hell.

"Then My people must continue to panic, and go, see, and hear the displays of sin and find more exciting ways to entertain their flesh, until the floods have destroyed everything inside their souls. The eyes and ears are never satisfied, and the gates of hell are never full.

"Why am I telling you this? So you will understand where My people are, and why they are hurting. My message will be for you to enable them to see why they are so full of fear and pride. The fear comes, because they have invited so much sin into their souls. The pride must protect that fear from being discovered. Fear and pride must disappear, before their souls can be rebuilt.

"The soul and heart are connected to the eyes and ears, giving the heart four windows to see and hear from. The tongue is the door, which opens into the soul. Once My people have opened the door with what they speak, then whatever is in the mind — the production they have created within their mind — will flood their souls when the words are spoken.

"My words will not return void and will be powerful over the mind. There are many strongholds in the mind — many doors in the theater of the mind for My people to hide their favorite pet demons behind. My words can penetrate all doors, but I have created My people to have a free will to choose what their desires will be. The parade of sin must be stopped from the viewing of My people's eyes and ears, and they must know My ways and My words, to fill their minds, until they begin to renew many rooms and open many doors into their minds.

"My people can be reached through the words of your testimony of what I have done for you. I am no respecter of persons, for I have chosen you to be a vessel of clay to show My people that there is hope and deliverance from the pits of hell, which is where they have placed themselves with not guarding their hearts.

"'How will people know when their hearts are guarded?' you ask.

"It will be when I have begun to be in every constant thought of their minds, and the parade of sin has stopped invading the windows of their souls.

"Oh, the parade has not stopped — only within that person's mind, who has yielded his mind, will, and emotions to My ways, and has continued to renew his mind with My words, and to create My images of love, joy, and peace within his own mind.

"The soul will begin to be restored, when the mind begins to seek more of Me, My words, and My people and begin to speak what I have done for them, by repeating the testimonies of what I have done for them.

"Fear not. I am telling you this for you to meditate on My words day and night, and to begin a fresh renewing of your mind. Listen to My voice, and listen to your voice when you speak; and you will know if your heart has been guarded or if you should repent, humble yourself, and turn away from the parade of sin, which will never stop.

"The demons of hell will not go away. The prince of this world, Satan himself, is like a roaring lion, seeking day and night to devour My people with his bright lights and worldly possessions of fun, pride of life, the power of ownership, and all the lusts to feed the flesh. Flesh will eat flesh, until it has eaten itself; then there will be nothing left.

"This day you must guard your heart from this hour forward and listen to My voice and your own voice to be sure we are speaking as one. Do not faint, for My ways are easy. You will never need to beg for bread or be concerned what the day will bring.

"I can hear My people's crying and their pain. The harvest is great, but the laborers' are few.

UNDERSTANDING THE FIVE-FOLD MINISTRY

Many of us have wondered, "Where is the power of God seen in the New Testament churches and the Azusa Street Church in Los Angeles, California, in the early 1900's?" Everyday occurrences in the early church included miraculous healings, vision and hearing restored, and people being set free from all kinds of oppression and depression. We hunger for it today!

The Bible gives us answers for all our questions about daily living. The answer to the above question is found in Ephesians 4:11-16:

"And He (Jesus) gave some apostles; and some, prophets; and some, evangelists; and some, pastors and teachers; for the perfecting of the saints, for the work of the ministry, for the edifying of the body of Christ: till we all come in the unity of the faith, and of the knowledge of the Son of God, unto a perfect man, unto the measure of the stature of the fullness of Christ: that we henceforth be no more children, tossed to and fro and carried about with every wind of doctrine, by the sleight of men, and cunning craftiness whereby they lie in wait to deceive; but speaking the truth in love, may grow up into Him in all things, which is the head, even Christ: from whom the whole body fitly joined together and compacted by that which every joint supplieth, according to the effectual working in the measure of every part, maketh increase of the body unto the edifying of itself in love." (KJV)

Jesus established the Five-Fold Ministry for the equipping and perfecting of the saints, and He calls those who are to fill the five positions of apostle, prophet, evangelist, pastor, and teacher in the body of Christ. These gifts are given by Jesus and are appointed by Him, not elected. The body of Christ needs the Five-Fold Ministry in place to prevent being deceived and to keep balance. Without these five gifts in place, power is greatly diminished. For example, a car engine running on only three cylinders has very little power, when it should be running on six cylinders.

When we understand the purpose for each of the five offices, we begin to understand why they are so important.

<u>Apostles</u> are sent with the authority to establish new churches, lay the foundation or truth, and function as special messengers, who will strengthen churches in practical teachings from the Word. Apostles minister with boldness, authority, and revelation. Their presence brings accountability, stability, and protection into the lives of believers, churches, and ministries. They confirm the call on certain believers' lives and have the authority to appoint elders and deacons.

Characteristically, apostles have a father's heart (to instruct, govern, love, nurture, encourage, admonish, and bring accountability). They have the spirit of humility and servanthood and operate with boldness in revelation knowledge and understanding of truths. Their relationship with God is very deep and their lives are examples. The Holy Spirit confirms the apostolic gift.

<u>Prophets</u> are front line warriors, watchmen, intercessors, guides, and guards of the body of Christ. They are God-minded, not interested in impressing people. Speaking under inspiration, prophets, also known as seers, are messengers for God, who have new dimensions of hearing in the spirit realm, foretelling events or hearing the human heart (memories, hurts, hopes, desires). Visions are a key function of the prophetic ministry. Prophets hate sin and will stand in the gap as intercessors. They rebuke, correct, judge, confirm and warn the body of Christ, often appearing impatient and confrontational. Their purpose is to confront the enemy and protect the sheep.

The characteristics of prophets include: great concern for purity of the church, times of isolation from others, strong gifts of discernment, operation in signs, wonders and miracles, and deep personal relationships with Father God. They are men and women of much prayer, walking in unusual authority, quick to perceive with keen alertness and perception, daring, very stern, moving people to obey. Prophets will point or guide the body of Christ God-ward. The office of the prophet is to be respected, protected, supported, and shielded.

<u>Evangelists</u> are the front-runners of the kingdom, blazing the trail for the sinner to repent. Their mandate is to gather (go and save souls), to recover, restore, and quicken to life. They have supernatural powers to meet and tackle the strongman and to discern evil spirits.

They are characteristically energetic, bold, forceful, courageous, global minded, outreach oriented, and grieved by hurting and suffering people.

<u>Pastors</u>, or shepherds, guard the sheep and officiate over the local body of believers. They are friends whose calm voice leads believers, guiding them through their Christian walk, the mainstays that stabilize the flock. Pastors officiate over baptism, communion, marriages, funerals, teaching, doctrine, and impartation of wisdom of the Lord to the flock.

The marks of true shepherds are: devotion to the flock, perseverance, the release of blessings, holy nurturing, attentiveness, nourishment, diligence in service, rescue of the lost and bound, faithful care, sheep gatherers, joy of freedom, and furnishers of security and protection. True pastors will never pull sheep from another herd.

<u>Teachers</u> ground believers: educating, instructing, and changing lives, behaviors, beliefs, and attitudes – equipping for ministry. With foresight and insight, their responsibility is to teach truth, life, holiness, salvation, and sanctification.

A teacher's personality is identified by: hunger for information, orderly thinking and use of visual aids, quickness to express needs, critical thinking, and grieving to see a failure.

Every part in the body of Christ is essential. God has arranged and placed each member, just as He desires. It is important for the members of the body to function in the place designed for each one (I Corinthians 12:18-31).

The Five-Fold Ministry must be brought back into the church, the body of believers. Then we shall begin to see many wonderful, powerful blessings come forth.

PART I

"This shall be a time to be sensitive to My voice and to know when I am speaking to you, and that when you speak, you shall speak My words and not your words, for I Am the one who will deliver My people from the ways of their flesh. You must be obedient to do what I tell you to do and when, so that your testimony will become the same as My testimony. We must be as one, just as you and your wife must be as one.

"You must be careful to include your wife with your testimony, for this is a vital part of your testimony, because it is not about you, nor is it about your wife. When you include your wife in your testimony, this takes the "I" out of your words, for then you will use the word "we" as being one; for as you and your wife are one, you must also include <u>God the Father</u>, <u>God the Son</u>, and the <u>Holy Spirit</u> to be as one with <u>you</u> and <u>your wife</u> – for then you will have the Five-Fold Ministry team in place (Genesis 2:21-24, <u>Ephesians 5:31-33</u>).

"I am about to teach you a new revelation knowledge about how powerful this can be for you to speak and talk as you go each day, to walk into the supernatural realm, and to know that you know that you will walk with a new level of boldness, and confidence, and will be clothed with humility for the equipping of the saints for the perfecting and purity and holiness. The Kingdom of God is at hand, and My Son is coming very soon. You must be very busy getting this message to My people, so they will begin to prepare for His coming at once.

UNDERSTANDING THE FIVE-FOLD MINISTRY

- Apostle   God the Father

- Prophet   Jesus the Son

- Evangelist   The Holy Spirit

- Pastor   The Husband

- Teacher   The Wife

PART II

"Go this day and know that I Am God, and I have given unto you knowledge, wisdom, and understanding for you to share with those who have ears to hear.

"People must be told and convinced that when they open the door to sin and allow the enemy to come into the theater of the mind, then they have given permission to the enemy – access to enter and to set up camp in the strongholds of the mind. The battle is taking place in the mind.

"This is why there must be a total renewing of the mind, and deliverance must take place before anything else can happen in the believer's life. The mind can control the window of the heart, and the tongue can control the soul. When the soul receives the final message, the body will do whatever the soul tells it to do, for the mind will continue to govern and rule and establish, just as the apostle works in the Five-Fold Ministry (Romans 8:5-7, Ephesians 2:1-3, Ephesians 4:23).

"The heart guides and points, as the windows of the heart are either open to the parade of sin or to the things of God, and will dictate what the tongue shall do; therefore it operates as the prophet in the Five-Fold Ministry to tell about past, present and future things to come, for the theater of the mind can present future dreams and visions to either see those things of darkness or light. The heart can be the deciding factor of how a person's life will be because of what is allowed into the four windows, brought in from the two eyes and two ears (Luke 6:45, Proverbs 27:19-20, John 7:38, Philippians 4:6-7, I John 3:21).

"The tongue, then, can be the evangelist. It can either gather, or it can scatter the body of believers or non-believers, as it is the rudder, which will determine which way the body shall move. When the tongue speaks death, then that is what shall appear. When the tongue speaks life, then that shall be done, as well. The power of the tongue must gather in the Five-Fold Ministry but can also scatter, if used in the flesh or the counterfeit of the Five Fold Ministry (Proverbs 12:18, Proverbs 15:1-4, Proverbs 18:21, James 3:5-6, Psalm 64:2-9, James 1:26, Job 6:25).

"When the tongue speaks, the door to the soul is open, and life or death will enter into the soul of the body, which will determine what the body shall do. The soul must be guarded, as the pastor guards the sheep, for when the sheep receive life, they shall do good things and bear fruit. When the sheep receive death, they shall do evil things; gossip, slander, division, and strife shall follow (Deuteronomy 11:18, Job 33:29-30, Psalm 63:1, Psalm 107:9, Proverbs 18:7, Proverbs 21:23, Acts 4:32, I Peter 2:11, Revelation 18:14).

"The body is made up with many members and will ultimately be driven as a result of mind (apostle), heart (prophet), tongue (evangelist); soul (pastor), for the body will show action and will become the teacher. People would rather see a sermon than hear one, for they have heard many

5

sermons by preachers, some good and some not so good. The body, then, has become the final product of acting out the sermon and has become the teacher to show people that whatever you are grounded in, you shall become. The power of the tongue will determine the final destination of the body (I Corinthians 6:19-20, I Corinthians 12, Luke 34:36, Romans 12:1-2).

"Your own personal temple of the Five-Fold Ministry must be equipped and ready for the perfecting of the saints. The apostle, which is the mind, must be clean, pure, and holy and govern the windows (eyes and ears) of the prophet, which is the heart, so it only receives clean, pure, and holy images.

"Then the evangelist, which is the tongue, will gather those hurting and wounded souls, who will be attracted by God's love and words of boldness and confidence and encouragement, yet clothed with humility, so many will come for salvation, healing, and deliverance.

"Then the pastor, which is the soul, must be guarded, as you will need to disciple and direct them to a full gospel church of believers, where the soul can be nurtured and receive good seed and grow.

"Then the teacher (the body) can go and do likewise and tell others to grow into the fullness, where their own personal temple can become a Five-Fold Ministry. Then they will duplicate themselves and pour out their life into others, and the body will be made whole and complete.

"God the Father is the one true God of the universe, and it is I who established everything in the beginning, for I have created man in My own image, as I am the Apostle of all apostles; just as I have given man a mind to be the apostleship over the body of man, which is My mobile temple to go from place to place. I have given man authority to set and establish churches, and to govern them, and to watch over them to keep them holy and pure before Me, to be sure man does not sit on the throne, that people do not have their eyes on man but are keeping their eyes on Me; so they will not stray away from the flock or listen to a strange voice and be led away to a path of destruction.

"God the Son, which is My Son, Jesus Christ, represents the prophet within the Five Fold Ministry, for My Son has a heart after the Apostle, God the Father, Maker and Creator of heaven and earth. My Son, Jesus Christ, the prophet within the supernatural Five-Fold Ministry, is the prophet within man's heart, for the Son only does what He sees The Father doing; therefore, the window to My Son's heart is pure and holy before Me and is without sin.

"My Son took all of the sins of the world and paid the ultimate price that no one should perish and be thrown into the lake of fire throughout eternity. My Son, Jesus, and the heart of man, and the prophet within the Five Fold Ministry must all three be as one, as the Holy Trinity is one.

"The Holy Spirit, which was sent to man when My Son came to Me, to prepare a place for men when the trumpet shall sound, represents the evangelist, for He will gather My people together unto salvation and the tongue of man must speak life and not death to bring My people into My Kingdom for the sake of the Gospel. The Holy Spirit, and the tongue of man, and the evangelist

within the Five Fold Ministry must be as one to represent how My people must be taught to be holy and pure, and to be ready for the day when My Son shall return, when the sound of the trumpet shall be heard in the heavenlies.

"The Holy Spirit is looking for souls and will cause a man's tongue to speak life into another person's life with the words of their testimony, announcing the purity and holiness of My Son; for the heart will cause that person to confess with his tongue, and his mouth will proclaim that My Son paid the price; for the mind will have believed to tell the heart that it is okay to profess with the tongue that Jesus Christ is Lord of their life.

"The <u>soul</u> of those who believe, which represents you, My son, as well as those who truly desire to receive the supernatural power of My Spirit, represents the <u>pastor</u>, as established for the Five Fold Ministry for the church. You are the pastor of your soul, and you must guard your soul to be sure it is pure and holy; as you search the apostle within your own mind to be sure it is in tune with God, the Heavenly Father.

"The Son shall be the prophet and will guide and point to the way and truth for everlasting life. When you are so close and focused with My Son in everything you do, then your heart will be pure, and the Holy Spirit will give you the words to speak, which will cause My people to bow before Me, and worship Me, and cry, 'Holy, holy, holy,' and to know I Am Lord of lords and King of kings, and to be ready to receive their heart's desire; for it will be what I desire for them.

"When the soul has been restored and filled with My purity, which has come from God the Father, the renewing of your mind as the apostle of your holy temple, and God the Son, the pure heart of man as the prophet of your holy temple, and the Holy Spirit, the tongue of man as the evangelist of your holy temple – then the <u>body</u> will follow the soul wherever it desires to be. The <u>body</u> will represent the <u>teacher</u> within the Five-Fold Ministry of the holy temple of God, which is what you must desire each and every day, as you seek to hear My voice, read, and study My Word."

UNDERSTANDING THE FIVE-FOLD MINISTRY

- God the Father   Apostle   The Mind

- Jesus the Son   Prophet   The Heart

- The Holy Spirit   Evangelist   The Tongue

- The Husband   Pastor   The Soul

- The Wife   Teacher   The Body

PART III

"Many times people hesitate to share any part of their life, because they do not believe that anything worthwhile has occurred in their lifetime. This is when you must remind them that first of all, they are very blessed to have been born in this country you live in, and that they are in their right mind. They have a place to sleep, and they have been able to eat. If they know the Lord as their Savior, then they are blessed beyond millions who do not know or have not received and are not walking daily by faith to become more like My Son.

"This is only the beginning to counting your many blessings, for then there is your health and every member of your body which is working properly, and the fact that you have children and grandchildren, and they are all healthy as well and have working members of their own bodies – for this is how the church of the living God must show the world. The world must see a healthy church, which is full of the joy of the Lord, and one that shows love for one another; one that is reaching out to those who are hurting and those who have needs.

"When people become so focused on their own lives and their own wants and needs instead of others, they are only feeding their own flesh. It will never satisfy what they are searching for – true fulfillment within their own lives. Many people have not experienced true maturity, where they no longer consider their own wants and desires, but are focused on a mission to accomplish touching others so their basic needs are met, and then they can go and do likewise and not be caught up with the materialism that the world has everyone caught up in, so that people cannot tell the difference between their needs or their wants.

"People need <u>air</u>, <u>food</u>, and <u>water</u>, and then <u>shelter</u> comes after they are <u>clothed</u>. These five basic needs are another Five Fold Ministry teaching to illustrate how much more complete, effective, and powerful life can be when these needs are explained within the structure of the Five Fold Ministry for the church to understand where they must focus, and how this can be a useful tool as an outreach to those around who are in need.

"<u>Air</u> is the apostle and is most essential, because it governs whether a person lives or not (even though oxygen is a drug and has limited purpose). Air must be present to have life (<u>Genesis 2:7</u>).

"<u>Food</u>, especially fruits which contain nutritious water and juices, points the way as in the Garden of Eden. The fruit, which was eaten, pointed the way out of the garden and set Adam and Eve's lives on a new course, as well as a new way of living, which meant ultimate death because of disobedience.

"The heart is the prophet to guide the way, just as Jesus is; so can food guide you to ultimate victory and long, healthy lives, or it can be most destructive to your bodies. This, then, makes food as a prophet used within the Five Fold Ministry realm of your understanding (Proverbs 23:21, Matthew 6:26, Acts 14:17, I Timothy 6:6-8).

"Now comes the evangelist, who gathers or scatters, who can do much good or much damage. You have learned about the tongue and the Holy Spirit of the Trinity as the evangelist. Now the water is the same, as well. The living water in the Bible refers to the blood of Jesus. The Holy Spirit as water can gather and carry people, places, and things and can be most useful, or most destructive as well, as it can gather or scatter (Luke 8:4, John 4:10-14, Ephesians 5:26, I John 5:8).

"Then comes the pastor, who guards as the soul guard, as the priest or head of the house guards the sheep. When you are clothed in your right mind with the humility of God, then you are a pastor of your body, the temple of the Holy Spirit, as clothing also guards and protects your body from the elements, as well as establishing boundaries to protect body parts from wandering eyes of the lust of the flesh (Genesis 3:7, Matthew 6:28-30, I Timothy 6:7-8, I Peter 5:5).

"Last is shelter, which represents the teacher, the human body, the place which must be guarded to ensure the outside elements or other sources cannot come and invade what must be taught within, and how the anointing can protect and keep, not only physical structures made of wood and mortar, or mental, or your own physical body, or the teacher, to prevent others from entering into the temple of your inner body structure, or the body of the church, or your own abode of physical shelter, representing the Holy of Holies, where the Spirit of the Lord will reside day and night to feel My Holy Presence forever" (Psalm 61:1-4, Psalm 91:1-2, John 2:21, I Corinthians 3:16-17, I Corinthians 6:19).

UNDERSTANDING THE FIVE-FOLD MINISTRY

- Apostle   Air

- Prophet   Food

- Evangelist   Water

- Pastor   Clothing

- Teacher   Shelter

PART IV

"You must never forget - the first thing you must always do is to awake with thanksgiving in your heart, to count your many blessings, and to rejoice in the Lord with the joy of the Lord unspeakable. This is why the joy of the Lord is unspeakable, because man cannot describe it with his own thoughts and words. Man must always have something to measure with to compare one thing to another, as joy is like a fulfilling of emptiness when the soul does not know what it is lacking; therefore joy can fill that void into something so awesome that it cannot be described.

"The joy of the Lord, which is unspeakable, is much greater than any man can put into words, for this kind of joy can only come from the Lord within the spirit of man; and it will keep him, protect him, and fill his soul to a level that man could never dream of experiencing in all of his wildest dreams.

"This day is that day when it is time to come unto Me, all those who are heavy with the worries and cares of this world, and to lay them down for the joy of the Lord. My joy can do exceedingly more abundantly than anything you can ever imagine in all of your wildest dreams.

"My people do not have this joy of the Lord, because they are trying to be happy with happenstance; in other words, whatever is happening in their life at any given time, or whatever their circumstance may be will determine how happy they are at each given instant.

"The joy of the Lord comes from within, and comes from knowing Me, and knowing who you are in Me, and releasing all of the cares, worries, and riches that this world has to offer for My joy unspeakable. It begins with starting to count your blessings, and to name them one by one, and to speak them out loud, until you are shouting from the top of your voice. You will begin to realize that you are alive and well. You must do this each and every day for the rest of your life, and then you will discover that I have chosen you to participate in this day and to go and share the joy and the good news of the Gospel to those who have ears to hear, and to invite them to go on a journey with the Father to set the captives free.

"This shall be a day to be filled with My joy unspeakable. Joy is omnipresent and is an apostle in the Five Fold Ministry (John 15:11, John 16:24, Philippians 2:2, I Peter 1:8).

"You must know that being full of My joy gives you strength, for this is truly the day I have made for you to rejoice and be glad in it; as you must be strong in the power of My might, which I have made available to you. Strength fills the position of prophet in the Five-Fold Ministry (Psalm 105:4, Isaiah 12:2, Nehemiah 8:10, Habakkuk 3:19, Mark 12:30).

"Be filled with boldness, as you must be a minister, or evangelist, of the gospel of Jesus Christ, and be a witness to those who are looking for someone who truly believes and is not afraid to share

the good news about the Kingdom of God. (Acts 4:13, Acts 4:31, Ephesians 3:12, Philippians 1:20)

"When you know that you know that you know who you are in Christ Jesus, you will walk in confidence and truly believe that you have been chosen and called to accomplish those things you know to do, and see yourself in the spiritual realm and not in the natural, but to see with spiritual eyes and ears of understanding with wisdom and knowledge, and walk in a faith walk like you have never known before, then you will begin to see the manifestations of My power. The pastor will be confident within his office to shepherd the sheep from among them, not above them (Philippians 1:25, Hebrews 3:6, I John 3:21, Ephesians 3:12, I John 2:28).

"Then those who have eyes to see and ears to hear will know that you are for real, clothed with My humility; that you are genuine, as you step into My steps, which have been ordered even before the foundation of this world and worlds yet to come. The office of teacher flows from a genuine, humble vessel. (Proverbs 15:33, Acts 20:19, I Peter 5:5)

"You must expect great things to happen, for you must be filled with My joy unspeakable, which shall be your strength, and be strong in my mighty power and be bold to speak the truth and walk in confidence to know who you are in Christ Jesus, yet be clothed with My humility, and then you will know what you must do, for you will be in My presence all the day long and the night time, too, for this is My heart's desire for you, as well as your heart's desire. Know this one thing I have just revealed to you and allow it to become so real in your life, that you know that you know with no fear, doubt, or unbelief.

"When you begin to believe the power of the spoken word and to know that power is within you and how quickly things can change in your life, as well as those lives around you, then you will be ready to receive those things which have been prepared and available for you on this day, as well as every day, while you are here on this earth and throughout eternity.

"Be ye ever so filled with My joy unspeakable to be an everlasting process as this will add many productive years unto your own life, as you already know how the enemy's primary mission is to steal your own joy, so your strength will no longer be, and you will become so easily intimidated by man and his manipulating ways, designed to rob you of your own confidence in what you were meant to think, say, or do. Then instead of My humility to clothe you, there will be fear which will want to rise up, when pride will be ever so quick to rise up and want to become a major part of your own life. Walk and talk with words of faith and assurance, as to know that you know the hope of your own calling in all things, so that nothing else shall matter unto you except to be in My everlasting presence all the day long and the night time as well.

UNDERSTANDING THE FIVE-FOLD MINISTRY

- Apostle   Joy

- Prophet   Strength

- Evangelist   Boldness

- Pastor   Confidence

- Teacher   Humility

PART V

"This shall begin another teaching of the Five-Fold Ministry, which you must share with those who have eyes to see and ears to hear with a supernatural understanding of where you must seek to go and flow as each day shall come forth.

"The first is the apostle, as mentioned in Ephesians 4:11-13; however the Creator is God Almighty, the Great I Am, and the one every single person must be accountable and committed to, for I am the Beginning and the End, and the Author and Finisher of everyone's life, which includes yours. You are descendants of Abraham, Isaac, and Jacob. This is something you must plant down deep within your spirit, so it will give you supernatural strength and power all of the days of your life here on earth and throughout eternity.

"You must believe that it is I, the Great I Am, who does the choosing, and I have chosen you, and those who hunger and thirst after righteousness shall be filled. I am no respecter of persons. What I shall do for one, I will do for you.

"I must caution you this day that this teaching is not intended to diminish the Five-Fold Ministries within the organized church body, but to enhance and to make stronger each one of these offices, which must be active in every fellowship of believers. There must always be an appointed leader and governing body of order, where man will be accountable to man and woman to woman; and the body must have freedom to praise and worship and enter into the Holy of Holies all the day long and to know there are no barriers to come between their own personal relationship with God the Father, God the Son, and the Holy Spirit, so that every believer can and shall have the supernatural power, which is made available, as they seek to walk in the Five Fold Ministry level.

"Now you shall know - God, apostle, mind, air and joy are the <u>Governing Function</u> to operate in life, and the correct order of life shall be God, air, mind, joy, then apostle to govern and establish man's priorities here on earth.

"The second shall be the <u>Guiding Function</u> to operate in life, beginning with Jesus, food, heart, strength, and prophet to point the way to truth and life everlasting.

"The third shall be the <u>Gathering Function</u> to operate in life, starting with the Holy Spirit, water, tongue, boldness, and the evangelist to bring new souls to the kingdom with love, joy, and excitement.

"The fourth function to operate in life is the Believer 1, whether married or single, the person who is the priest and headship of the home, <u>Guarding Function</u>, beginning with Believer 1, then clothing, soul, confidence, and the pastor, who shall guard and watch over those they are responsible for, to be a covering and protection with love, truth, knowledge, and understanding.

15

"The last, but not least, <u>Grounding Function</u>, shall be Believer 2, the spouse of Believer 1, or helpmate, or friend; or the single person alone could operate in both offices, until time shall change this situation. Believer 2, the shelter, physical body, humility of God, and the teacher is the life function which will show those who are believers, as well as nonbelievers, a real live demonstration of how the power can operate when all of the above are in full operation.

"All of these mentioned above must operate within the boundaries of <u>Love</u>, which is the glue to hold these together. The nine fruit of the Spirit must be evident in every believer's life. There must be a true repentance and a turning away from those works of the flesh, to die daily, and to become a new creature in Christ Jesus, as you continue to journey with the Father to set the captives free and to become free indeed."

UNDERSTANDING THE FIVE-FOLD MINISTRY

- Governing Function   Apostle

- Guiding Function   Prophet

- Gathering Function   Evangelist

- Guarding Function   Pastor

- Grounding Function   Teacher

PART VI

Lord, help my belief to become so strong that I shall walk in the Gift of Faith with such power and with such boldness and confidence that I will be able to believe and shall not doubt within my heart for all mountains to be removed from my life, as they appear as many obstacles as opportunities for growth, and there shall be those many times when I shall speak, and they shall move as though nothing else matters, and I shall <u>feel</u> (apostle), <u>see</u> (prophet), <u>hear</u> (evangelist), <u>smell</u> (pastor), and <u>taste</u> (teacher) the power of God, and know that it is the true manifestation of God's awesome power.

"I will say to you that you have just received another teaching for the Five-Fold Ministry; for I shall give it to you, so that you will understand and begin to share this with those who are ready to receive.

"The <u>apostle</u> is to <u>feel</u>, for it is omnipresent as air, joy, mind; so to feel or sense danger, or joy, or humility, heaviness, or lightness, in the air, as to <u>feel</u> shall govern what a substance may be made of. To feel a certain way may determine if you wish to examine closer (<u>Exodus 10:21</u>).

"The <u>prophet</u> is known as a 'seer', or to <u>see</u> into the present or future and to know about certain things in a person's life, or into the heavenlies, as to what to expect in the future (<u>2 Samuel 24:11-12</u>, 2 Kings 17:13, Isaiah 30:10, Matthew 11:4-5, Luke 24:39).

"The <u>evangelist</u> must be able to <u>hear</u> from God and to deliver a timely message in such a way so those who are present are able to <u>hear</u>; for the Gospel message shall be preached in several different ways at one time, so those who have ears to hear shall have the opportunity to respond, for they have been presented a new fresh method of the Gospel, which will cause them to respond like they have never known before (Matthew 11:15, Mark 4:24, John 5:25, John 10:27, <u>Revelation 4:1</u>).

"The <u>pastor</u> must <u>smell</u> like the sheep, for he shall spend many long days and nights with them, and the sheep will know the sound of the pastor's voice. The pastor shall smell like the sheep from the close association with them over long periods of time (John 10:3, John 21:17, <u>2 Corinthians 2:15-17</u>, Ephesians 5:1-2).

"The <u>teacher</u> must learn to <u>taste</u>, as babies begin to learn by putting everything they find into their mouths. This is one of the first rules of learning to see if they like something or not - to taste it and see if it is worth eating. Then later, they begin to smell, then hear, and see, and feel (or sense) other areas of their life, as they progress and continue to learn more as time permits them to continue on the journey with their Father and to become free indeed, and then to invite others to come along, either in the physical or the natural, and to become free as well" (<u>Psalm 34:8</u>).

UNDERSTANDING THE FIVE-FOLD MINISTRY

- Apostle   Feel

- Prophet   See

- Evangelist   Hear

- Pastor   Smell

- Teacher   Taste

PART VII

"This is a day to be calm and to know that all is well in this season, for you must not look at those things which are taking place in the natural as something you must react toward, but instead to evaluate and to see beyond what has happened, and what it will take to make things better in the future:

- to determine who (Ephesians 4:17-24, Proverbs 3:3-6, Proverbs 4:20-22) shall be involved;

- what part (Romans 12: 3-8, I Corinthians 12: 11, Ephesians 4:7-16) should each one play, as the body must function as one;

- and to also know why (Ephesians 4:30-32, I Corinthians 2:12-16, Luke 11:9-13) some things are the way they are and why they are not, for it will not be necessary to change all things and everything at one time;

- except to know where (Ezekiel 34:1-31, I Peter 5:1-4) each person fits;

- and what part they shall participate in to make the body as one, to operate ever so smoothly as one, for there shall be a special time and place when (Ecclesiastes 3:12, Habakkuk 2:2-3) these things will need to happen.

"You will have no need to become upset or consumed with who, what, why, where, and when, for these five shall operate as a function of the Five-Fold Ministry.

"It shall be ever so important, as you continue to search out who is really operating as the apostleship of one's life. Many times, it is believed to be God the Father, when in reality, it is a familiar spirit who wants to operate as that entity to portray that image. That spirit can be so deceptive to even the one within that thought life, operating within the mind.

"The what (prophet) shall continue to guide and direct, but it must be firmly planted within the mind to know who (apostle) has established all things from the very beginning, and to believe that the Son has total dominion with what (prophet) is said and done.

"Then there is the question why (evangelist) some things happen the way they do and some do not, for the Holy Spirit shall determine those areas of goodness, mercy, and grace; as the spirit of darkness shall use others to cause confusion in every situation.

"The where (pastor) must operate in its proper position to guard and protect those who are walking within the umbrella of My protection.

"Then you will know <u>when</u> (teacher) all things are in their proper position and time. Nothing else shall matter except to go onward and upward in a forward motion, just as an advancing army shall continue to move, possess new lands and new expanded territories, take those people captive who are not aware of their own bondage, and to bring them out of that spiritual darkness into the marvelous light of My love, mercy and grace.

"Know this one thing, how this teaching can become far more in depth. You must use this as a guideline for a true and healthy discipleship program, as you continue to strengthen and stretch and to enlarge your own territories. Many who say they are going here and there for the work of the kingdom may be on the right and straight course of action, or they may be causing more disharmony and confusion to the body."

UNDERSTANDING THE FIVE-FOLD MINISTRY

- Apostle   Who

- Prophet   What

- Evangelist   Why

- Pastor   Where

- Teacher   When

PART VIII

"Many will come alongside to work with and help you; yet may you be ever so alert and watchful, as cautious, to insure man does not try to control or limit My plans and My ways; as there shall be no Big I's and little you's, but a chain of command which will be established within the Kingdom. The servant of all shall be the most fit for leadership. It shall be done, by example, in group and team effort. The focus shall not be upon one man or woman, but upon the one and only Commander and Chief, Jesus Christ, the Son of the Living God of Abraham, Isaac, and Jacob.

"May you be ever so yielded, with such a total surrender unto Me, the Lord your God: <u>Creator</u> (Genesis 1:27, Ecclesiastes 12:1, I Peter 4:19), <u>Savior</u> (Isaiah 43:3), <u>Deliverer</u> (2 Samuel 22:2, Psalm 18:2, Romans 11:26), <u>Provider</u> (Job 38:41, Psalm 65:9, Luke 12:20), and <u>Leader</u> (Psalm 22:2, 3, Romans 2:4) as to meet every need (emotional, physical, and spiritual).

"This shall comprise of a new Five-Fold Ministry team of ultimate leadership, with a Trinity God Head of sorts, giving you new and practical tools with which you will be able to reach a new generation. This will become a new, yet creative, way to reach, and comfort, and convince those who have never been exposed to any type of true identity or have not come under any true and everlasting authority, where faith and grace shall be as foreign unto them as so many other religious terms; yet they will need to be exposed unto a power greater than themselves.

"This will be called many things by most. It will create such a fear, because it shall include a complete and total surrender unto everything they ever trusted, yet did not understand; while all along the way, it will ultimately end up in dying unto self and the flesh, to serve others.

"My ways are to become so very real and true unto you, as you must know and learn all the more to be still and listen to hear what the Spirit is saying to the church body as a unity, not divided among itself, but to be as one with Me."

UNDERSTANDING THE FIVE-FOLD MINISTRY

- Apostle   Creator

- Prophet   Savior

- Evangelist   Deliverer

- Pastor   Provider

- Teacher   Leader

PART IX

"May you be ever so grateful in this very hour and day, as to know that you know, as you have seen My power at work in your own life. Then so shall you be able to see how there is still so much more available for others to see, and experience, and enjoy; just as you will continue to be a part of such a move of My Spirit like most will never see in an entire lifetime.

"Walk with Me and talk with Me in such a way as if to say, 'OK, Lord. Here we are, willing, and ready, and available to go wherever you say and to stay as long as it shall take,' then to go when it is time to another place, and then to another, until such time, when you will be able to go into a place of refuge, rest, and relaxation; so you will be restored <u>emotionally</u>, <u>mentally</u>, <u>physically</u>, <u>spiritually</u>, and <u>financially</u>, for these five shall become an integral part of a Five-Fold Ministry maintenance plan, where you will need to be aware in all of these areas in all of your affairs; so you will be most effective to do the work of the ministry of the Gospel. You will then be able to accomplish those tasks at hand, so that others will be ever so blessed in your own coming and going, enhancing and advancing the Kingdom of God.

"Speak life into every situation and/or circumstance, no matter how things may appear to be in the natural. Do not allow the enemy even one minute to speak into your ear; for then, it will suddenly become a nightmare or even worse; for once you have entertained a single negative thought, then you have opened the door, and the enemy will walk right inside and convince you of thoughts and words beyond your own imagination. Suddenly you will find those words becoming actions to exceed far beyond where you would ever believe to be possible.

"Now is the time and this is the day to draw closer to Me than ever before, singing and speaking words of affirmation about who you are in Me, and Me living inside of you; as the two shall become as one, bound ever so jointly together as a five-strand cord, unable to be broken, with <u>God the Father</u>, <u>God the Son</u>, <u>the Holy Spirit</u>, <u>yourself</u>, and <u>your spouse</u>, all inter-woven, becoming as one, unable to be broken - <u>emotionally</u>, <u>mentally</u>, <u>physically</u>, <u>financially</u>, and <u>spiritually</u>."

MAINTENANCE PLAN – FIVE-FOLD MINISTRY

- God the Father   Emotionally

- Jesus the Son   Mentally

- The Holy Spirit   Physically

- Husband   Financially

- Wife   Spiritually

PART X

"You are asking Me this moment, 'What about the Five-Fold Ministry of the world?' to help people understand how the equipping of the world is doing a much better job than the churches, although the church is the one who should possess all the power of the kingdom, so the world shall not dominate the churches of today.

"I will say to you this day, you must conduct a teaching of this very concept of comparison teaching; so those who are in the world can see inside the church, and those in the church will be able to understand the world, and how it has united to such a degree, using <u>money</u>, <u>sex</u>, <u>power</u>, <u>love</u>, and <u>communication with education</u>. This shall make up the Five Fold system for the world's standards; for without the flow of money, nothing happens within this world.

"People have learned to worship money as their God the Father, as they have sold out the whole route to what money can do for them and their family. Many people are willing to die for the love of money, or the power, which they feel money will bring into their life.

"<u>Money</u> is the apostle of the world, as it governs everything the world considers to be most important.

"<u>Sex</u> is a strong driving force, which can guide people into a state of utter destruction or everlasting pleasure, and can also be a warning and correction tool to be used in the world. Many men and women alike have fallen into this trap, prophesying the future for those things to come, as the prophet of the world.

"<u>Power</u>, like money and sex, follows as the manifestation of the world trinity of money, sex, and power. These three have changed the course of history throughout all times. Countries and people have been destroyed and ruled by these three elements.

"The world uses <u>love</u> and acceptance, in most instances, better than the church to pastor those who have real physical needs and to put feet on prayers to actually do something, instead of preaching about it or talking about it.

"<u>Communication</u> is the real tool of today to teach those who need to be taught and to help others know what is going on around them, and next door, and all around the world. People are truly like sheep, so easily led astray to those places where they need not go to be slaughtered, because they do not understand the principles and powers of this world nor of the worlds to come; so therefore, everyone must be given this message so they, too, will understand what is happening in their life, for they must know, 'Who are they on a journey with this day. Is it the father of lies, or the Father of truth?'"

THE FIVE-FOLD OF THE WORLD

- Apostle   Money

- Prophet   Sex

- Evangelist   Power

- Pastor   Love

- Teacher   Communication with
                   Education

THE FINAL HOUR

God is looking for yielded vessels with a burden for lost souls, dedicated worshippers, and committed intercessors (prayer warriors).

"Jesus loves you so much that He gave his life, so no one shall perish, no not one, and so they can know Him, as well, and have an everlasting relationship with Him. Never again will they need to feel alone, or rejected, or that no one cares if they exist or not. They are not an accident waiting for something to happen, for their life has a definite plan, and a purpose, and destiny for someone else, other than themselves.

"Know this! When My Son died on the cross for you, He not only had you on his mind, but thousands of others as well; for there are many who must come to the knowledge, wisdom, and understanding of how important each life is to the Master Creator.

"I Am that I Am, and there shall be no other gods before Me this day or any other day, for all of the days of your life and throughout eternity.

"You have spoken, as you have heard it spoken and sung from others, that every knee shall bow and every tongue shall confess that Jesus Christ is Lord. He is the King of kings and Lord of lords, and you must recognize His Presence and His Glory."

FIVE-FOLD MINISTRY

LOVE IS THE GLUE THAT HOLDS IT ALL TOGETHER

GOVERNING FUNCTIONS	GOD THE FATHER	AIR	MIND	JOY	APOSTLE	FEEL	WHO
GUIDING FUNCTIONS	JESUS THE SON	FOOD	HEART	STRENGTH	PROPHET	SEE	WHAT
GATHERING FUNCTIONS	HOLY SPIRIT	WATER	TONGUE	BOLDNESS	EVANGELIST	HEAR	WHY
GUARDING FUNCTIONS	SPOUSE 1	CLOTHING	SOUL	CONFIDENCE	PASTOR	SMELL	WHERE
GROUNDING FUNCTIONS	SPOUSE 2	SHELTER	BODY	HUMILITY	TEACHER	TASTE	WHEN

	Team of Ultimate Leadership Trinity Godhead	Maintenance Plan	Five-Fold Ministry of the World
GOVERNING FUNCTIONS (Cont'd)	CREATOR	MENTALLY	MONEY
GUIDING FUNCTIONS (Cont'd)	SAVIOR	EMOTIONALLY	SEX
GATHERING FUNCTIONS (Cont'd)	DELIVERER	PHYSICALLY	POWER
GUARDING FUNCTIONS (Cont'd)	PROVIDER	SPIRITUALLY	LOVE
GROUNDING FUNCTIONS (Cont'd)	LEADER	FINANCIALLY	COMMUNICATION WITH EDUCATION

"Speak life into every situation and/or circumstance, no matter how things may appear to be in the natural. Do not allow the enemy even one minute to speak into your ear; for then it will suddenly become a nightmare or even worse; for once you have entertained a single negative thought, then you have opened the door, and the enemy will walk right inside and convince you of thoughts and words beyond your own imagination; so suddenly, you will find those words becoming actions to exceed far beyond where you would never believe to be possible.

"Go forth in this very day and hour, knowing the power source of creation within your very own <u>mind</u>, and how it distributes seed to be planted within the <u>heart</u> to be cultivated and to grow; so that as the mind thinketh, therefore it is created to be nurtured and to produce an abundant crop, which shall begin to flow, as to overflow, out of the <u>mouth</u>, entering into the <u>soul</u> of man, producing such an everlasting image, setting into motion and action which the <u>body</u> will not be able to deny; therefore, the cycle of life shall continue upon its course of action, which was originally birthed and created within the mind.

"Believe and receive all that there is to be in this life, as well as the next, while reading My Text, standing upon all of those promises, which you know are both real and true for you, as well as others, who will come unto Me with true Godly sorrow, with a true repentant heart, with such a hunger and thirst to be reconciled and restored into My Presence.

"Look into the future as being so bright, even in the midst of gloom and doom, which most are assuming to come; yet, while true, you will know what to do, as you will not have your own trust and confidence set upon man's view and ideas with what to do, but, instead, your own total trust and confidence will be set upon Me, the Lord your God, which shall be your only help in time of trouble. Trust solely and wholly and completely in Me, the Lord your God; as you shall continue to be still and listen; then to hear with clarity of vision, knowing <u>who</u> you are, <u>what</u> you must do, and <u>why</u>; then to know <u>where</u> to go and <u>when</u>, while continuing to pray without ceasing, being ever so careful to not panic or to run ahead, trying to help Me out, but instead to STOP (stay there – obtain peace). Wait upon Me, the Lord your God, as you shall mount up with wings as eagles, to run and not be weary, and to walk and not faint.

"Now is the time, and this is the day to draw closer to Me than ever before, singing and speaking words of affirmation about who you are in Me, and Me living inside of you; as the two shall become as one – bound ever so jointly together as a 5-strand cord, unable to be broken, with <u>God the Father</u>, <u>God the Son</u>, <u>The Holy Spirit</u>, <u>yourself</u>, and <u>your spouse</u>, all interwoven, becoming as one, unable to be broken <u>emotionally</u>, <u>mentally</u>, <u>physically</u>, <u>financially</u>, and <u>spiritually.</u>

NINE FRUIT OF THE SPIRIT

Galatians 5:22-23: "But the fruit of the Spirit is love, joy, peace,
longsuffering, gentleness, goodness, faith, meekness, temperance:
against such there is no law." KJV

A single-minded lifestyle is produced in God's people as they allow the Spirit to direct and influence their lives, destroying the power of sin, especially the works of the flesh, and walk in fellowship with God. The Spirit and the flesh are opposites, resulting in fierce and unrelenting conflict within us as Christians. We cannot be victorious by our own strength (Romans 7:15-23). Only the Holy Spirit can produce the fruit of the Spirit.

The fruit of the Spirit is one and indivisible; the works of the flesh are plural. When the Spirit fully controls the life of a believer, they display all of these graces. The first three (the Trinity of the fruit of the Spirit) concern our attitude toward God; the second three involves social relationships; the third group lists principles that guide a Christian's conduct.

****

"May you be all the more yielded unto My will and My ways than ever before; so then you will be all the more convinced and committed in so many areas of your own life that you never dreamed to be possible before now.

"Know this one thing, how you must walk in such divine <u>love</u>, <u>joy</u>, and <u>peace</u> with each and every moment of every day, with such an attitude of gratitude, with singing and dancing, being ever so true unto Me and My ways, as well as unto your own self, not being weighted down or heavy burdened with life past, present, or future, but counting your many blessings, naming them one by one out loud; so that your own soul may rejoice and be glad, seeking that glorious peace, which surpasses all human understanding.

"Go forth in this very day and hour, waiting ever so patiently upon Me, the Lord your God, as to be still and listen and hear My voice speaking to you. Come with Me to a new place, where you have never been before, knowing all the while long how there is still yet so much more in store.

"Sing a new song. Dance a new step. Speak life with such words of power, allowing My <u>love</u>, <u>joy</u>, and <u>peace</u> to flow out of your own mouth like a flood, producing a mighty river with such power and force to create electricity, with the ability to light up everything in its path that is not willing to take the ride, because it will get rough, and bumpy, and cold, and wet, and lonely in some places, while on this journey; yet you must go and know that the right way is not always easy and smooth, unless you have made up your mind to totally yield, and surrender, and give it all up to Me, the Lord your God, not looking back or trying to hold on to something or anything, which may hinder you to come and go with Me on this exciting journey with Me.

"Allow My <u>joy unspeakable</u> to saturate your very soul ever so deep from within; so that, while you are so very busy being grateful with everything within you, then so will you **feel** a river of life swelling up inside, deep within your soul, like a mighty river of water rising up ever so high and wide, flowing outside of its own natural banks; so that suddenly you will then **see** how you come to a new place with a new sound, as you will begin to **hear** and see with new ears and eyes of understanding; so that nothing will be able to stop you from **smelling** the awesome fragrance of My sweet aroma, while you will also be able to **taste** the absolute goodness of My <u>love</u>, <u>mercy</u>, and <u>grace</u>.

"Come unto Me in this day and very hour, with such a complete and total <u>peace</u>, as to rest with Me in all things, which you shall think, say, or do, knowing all the while long how there is so much more still yet to come.

"Speak out loud the desires of your own heart, knowing full well the purpose and intentions of your own heart, so there will be noting left unsaid or undone; for you will be certain to find a complete and total <u>peace</u>, which shall surpass all of your own natural human understanding.

"Be ye not conformed to those things of this world, knowing how you are an alien or a stranger, possessing and claiming everywhere your feet shall touch, believing and receiving the blessings of the Lord God Almighty. Go forth in this very day and very hour, as to experience My power to flow continually within you and through you; so you will be a blessing into everyone's life.

"Many have come and gone over so many years with days of nights of trials and toilings of every kind you could ever imagine; but somehow, they were unable to master the art of resting and trusting in Me all the more, knowing how there is so much power available and ready to be released, once my <u>love</u>, <u>joy</u>, and <u>peace</u> is caught and demonstrated, in such a way so then My <u>longsuffering</u>, <u>gentleness</u>, and <u>goodness</u> can become known and recognized as a most powerful attribute, as well.

"Then, and only then, will My <u>faith</u> become all it was meant to be, standing tall in the midst of giant oak trees and redwoods, reaching toward the heavens in such a magnificent way, like no man has ever known, bringing about such strength with <u>meekness</u> and <u>temperance</u> with such refining and defining, with answers to so many unanswered questions, many of which man could not comprehend to ask."

****

1. Love

The Bible defines love as a loyal, steadfast, unselfish, freely given love, including a love for the poor, the underprivileged, strangers, and our enemies, a caring and seeking for the highest good of another person without motive for personal gain. Without love, no matter what gifts operate through us, we are nothing and will have no reward (1 Corinthians 13:2).

2. Joy

Supernatural joy comes to the believer who counts our many blessings out loud every day, reminding ourselves to be grateful. Joy is not a grin we put on when someone is watching us, nor is it just a happy feeling. It is far more than just having fun.

Joy is an active delight in the promises and nearness of God to those who love Jesus Christ. Joy keeps us from self-pity, even in times of trial, suffering, and persecution.

3. Peace

More than absence of conflict, more than quietness and rest, the Bible teaches that peace is full of life, including health, wholeness, harmony, and well-being between us and our heavenly Father. We must recognize our need for real fellowship with each other, the unity spoken of in the Book of Ephesians.

4. Longsuffering

Endurance, patience, and being slow to anger or despair helps us to learn together, forgive mistakes without limit, and keeps us from being critical of one another. We are to love those who don't love us back, those who are different from us.

5. Gentleness

Gentleness flows from a genuine concern for others. It is free of arrogance and is never manipulative or authoritarian, never wanting to inflict pain. There is no limit to wanting to help others, protecting and encouraging their gifts and ministries.

6. Goodness

A zeal for truth and righteousness and a hatred for evil can be expressed in acts of goodness (Luke 7:37-50) or in rebuking and correcting evil in love.

7. Faith

Because of God's pattern of faithfulness, we know He will carry out His plan, and Jesus will come back to fulfill all He has promised. By our firm and unswerving loyalty and adherence to God, we build relationships with each other and are not dependent on circumstances. We are united by promise, commitment, trustworthiness, and honesty.

8. Meekness (teachable)

Restraint coupled with strength and courage, meekness describes a person who can be angry when anger is needed and humbly submissive when submission is needed.

9. Temperance (self control)

Having control over our own desires and passions, including faithfulness to our marriage vows, means that we will not allow our weaknesses to keep us from obeying God and His Word. We are not our own; we were bought with a price.

The fruit of the Spirit exemplify the character of Jesus.

THE WORKS OF THE FLESH

Galatians 5: 16-26: "This I say then, Walk in the Spirit,
and ye shall not fulfill the lust of the flesh.
For the flesh lusteth against the Spirit,
and the Spirit against the flesh:
and these are contrary the one to the other:
so that ye cannot do the things that ye would.
But if ye be led by the Spirit, ye are not under the flesh.

"Now the works of the flesh are manifest, which are these:
adultery, fornication, uncleanness, lasciviousness,
idolatry, witchcraft, hatred, variance, emulations,
wrath, strife, seditions, heresies, envying, murders,
drunkenness, revellings, *and such like:*
of the which I tell you before, as I have also told you in the past,
they that do such things shall not inherit the kingdom of God." KJV

The works of the flesh are easy to recognize and may be listed as sexual sins (the first four), sins connected with pagan religion (the next two), sins of temper (the next nine), and sins of drunkenness (the last two).

1. Adultery

Voluntary sexual relations by a married person with someone other than their spouse.

2. Fornication

Unlawful sexual relations, including adultery; taking pleasure in pornography: pictures, films, or writing.

3. Uncleanness

Sexual sins, evil deeds, and vices, including thoughts and desires planted in our hearts; ceremonially impure (Ephesians 5:3).

4. Lasciviousness

Sensuality, or following one's passions and desires to the point of having no shame or public decency (2 Corinthians 12:21).

5. Idolatry

Worship of idols; excessive devotion to or reverence for some person or thing, greater than our love for God.

6. Witchcraft

Sorcery, spiritism, black magic, and worship of demons and use of drugs to produce "spiritual" experiences; bewitching attraction or charm.

7. Hatred

Intense, hostile intentions and acts; extreme dislike or enmity.

8. Variance

Quarreling, antagonism, a struggle for superiority (Romans 1:29).

9. Emulations

Resentfulness or envy of another's success; ambitious rivalry (Romans 13:13).

10. Wrath

Explosive anger or rage, fury, which flares into violent words and deeds, especially for punishment or vengeance (Colossians 3:8).

11. Strife

Selfish ambition, seeking of power, contention, or competition (2 Corinthians 12:20).

12. Seditions

Introducing divisive teachings not supported by the Word of God (Romans 16:17).

13. Heresies

Division within the body of believers into selfish groups or cliques, which destroy the unity of the body of Christ (I Corinthians 11:19), the rejection of a belief that is part of church dogma.

14. Envyings

Resentful dislike of another person who has something that one desires.

15. Murders

The act of killing a person unlawfully and with malice.

16. Drunkenness

Impairing one's mental or physical control by alcoholic drink.

17. Revellings

Excessive party spirit, involving alcohol, drugs, sex, or the like.

GIFTS OF THE SPIRIT FOR BELIEVERS

I Corinthians 12:4-11: There are diversities of gifts, but the same Spirit.
There are differences of ministries, but the same Lord.
And there are diversities of activities,
but it is the same God who works all in all.

But the manifestation of the Spirit is given to each one for the profit of all:
*for to one is given the **word of wisdom** through the Spirit,*
*to another the **word of knowledge** through the same Spirit,*
*to another **faith** by the same Spirit,*
*to another **gifts of healing** by the same Spirit,*
*to another the **working of miracles**,*
*to another **prophecy**,*
*to another **discerning of spirits**,*
*to another **different kinds of tongues**,*
*to another the **interpretation of tongues**.*

But one and the same Spirit works all these things,
distributing to each one individually as He wills." KJV

The manifestation of the Holy Spirit occurs through a variety of spiritual gifts given to believers (1Corinthians. 12:4-11), intended for the lifting up and sanctification of the church, and are different than the gifts and ministries listed in Romans 12:6-8 and Ephesians 4:11 that give the power and ability to minister to believers in the body. They tell of the ministries of apostles, prophets, evangelists, pastors, and teachers, chosen by the Lord, taken captive by Him, and given by Him to the body of Christ. Their ministry is meant to bring believers to a maturity where each can receive gifts and contribute to the body. They are a part of God's design, as He has set the various parts of the human body in their place to fulfill their proper function to promote life (1 Corinthians 12:18, 28). The gifts were given for the Church Age, and not until Jesus comes again will they be ended, or no longer necessary.

If the believer eagerly desires the manifestations of the Spirit, they are given according to the will of the Spirit, as He determines the need. Some gifts may be manifested on a regular basis, and there may be more than one gift given, if needed. We as believers should seek more than one gift (1 Corinthians12;31).

Just because someone operates in a spectacular gift, we should never believe that person is more spiritual than we, nor should we assume that God approves of all the person does or teaches. Spiritual gifts are not to be confused with the fruit of the Spirit.

Word of wisdom. This is a wise utterance spoken through the operation of the Holy Spirit's divine counsel, applying the Holy Spirit's message of wisdom to a specific situation or problem

(Act 6:10; 15:13-22), giving an adequate portion of insight to a specific need. The wisdom of God for daily living is obtained by study and meditation of God's Word, by prayer, and by divine revelation.

"The more you go to see My people,
The more you realize how they hunger to be heard.
They need to know My love for them;
They need to hear a word,
A word of encouragement to know that I'm not mad;
How the angels in Heaven shall rejoice and truly be glad
When just one will turn away
From the wicked path of destruction
And know that all is well this day.
"Everyone's under construction.
The temples must be restored, and new ones created, too,
For there are many out there, just like you,
Who wanted to go ahead and get the job started.
Waiting on Me was sounding so retarded.
People around you were saying things like,
'God helps those who help themselves.'
Little did they know about all the little elves,
Who were only too happy to lead them astray
To a path of sure destruction – to guide them all the way."

Word of knowledge. Inspired by the Holy Spirit, this utterance reveals knowledge concerning people, circumstances, or Biblical truth, often connected closely with prophecy (Acts 5:1-10; 1 Corinthians 14:24-25). This gift gives the supernatural ability to receive and share revealed knowledge that was not otherwise known, or the ability to gather and clarify large quantities of biblical knowledge with unusual spiritual insight.

"I will say to you, My precious son and daughter,
The path I have chosen for you is to walk across the water.
You've stepped in the water, and you've gone a little deeper
Until it's over your head, and you've swam in the river.
The river of life will take you to the sea,
Where people are waiting on the other side for you and Me.
When they see you walking across the water,
They'll say, 'Watch out! This can't be!'
For they'll know who you are standing by – Me!
For it is I, the Lord your God, who will be standing next to you,
And the demons will tremble. I will be in plain view,
For they shall scatter, looking for a place to go,
And truth and light shall reveal! Everyone shall know!
The time of My coming is very soon, you see.
You must not delay to tell them about Me.

Many have been deceived!
They say, 'Oh, I believe,'
And they know it's a lie;
So tell them your testimony and invite them inside.
The time is now for the truth to prevail.
The games are over. There are no more stories to tell.
People are hungry and thirsty to hear the truth.
Don't make it so easy! Never give up,
When you know they don't know. It's time to fill their cup.
"Fill their cup with My love that never fails to win
And invite them to come in to remove all their sin.

"Go this day on a journey and a mission
And be filled with joy and strength, not with malnutrition.
The Gospel is the good news to set all men free.
Be free indeed, so all can see the joy in you and Me."

Gift of faith. Not to be confused with saving faith, a special, supernatural faith is given by the Holy Spirit that enables us to believe God for the miraculous and supernatural – faith that moves mountains (1 Corinthians 13:2), usually in combination with the gift of healing or miracles.

"You're hearing My voice as you go each day,
And you will soon realize that I have much to say.
It's when you listen, and when you pray
As you go on this journey – not to have your way
But to do My will, which is My plan for you,
To protect you, and prosper you, and to bring you through
All of those places, where many will never go,
Because fear and pride has them in so much in bondage. I know you know.
Don't be alarmed, and don't panic. We have just begun
To walk into a new place, to do things never done.
At least you can say to your children someday,
'I've walked with God, and He's lead me along the way.'

"I'll never leave you this day or the next.
You know it's true. It's in the text.
You have many questions – for I know you very well.
You're saying, 'OK, Lord. I know it's hard to tell.'

"You know that walking by faith is the only way
To grow and mature, as you go along each day."

Gifts of healings. These gifts are given to restore physical health by divinely supernatural means (Matthew 4:23-25; 10:1; Acts 3:6-8; 4:30). Every act of healing is a special gift of God. Although the gift of healing is not given to every member of the body, all members may pray for the sick. God is the healer, and He alone must receive the glory (Acts 3:12-16, Exodus 15:26). When faith is present, the sick will be healed. The Spirit will also encourage an atmosphere of faith, love, and acceptance that will help the sick person to receive. Healing may also occur as a result of obedience to instructions in James 5:14-16.

"Know the time is coming soon for My bride-to-be.
The church must be ready – no spot or wrinkle – you see.
The blood will cover them all as white as snow,
If only they will repent and know that they know
Each one has been bought with a price
One cannot imagine. Be sure you tell them about the sacrifice
That was paid in full that day on Calvary.

"All sins were forgiven, so all can become free:
Free to be forgiven and to begin a new life:
Free from sorrow and shame, and sickness and pain,
To heal the lame; so the blind can see.
Life is filled with miracles for all to believe.
Just believe and receive it this special day,
And see how many miracles will come your way."

Miracles. The working of miracles is the special ability that God gives to certain members of the body of Christ to serve as human intermediaries through whom it pleases God to perform powerful acts that are perceived by observers to have altered the ordinary course of nature during these manifestations of supernatural power, including divine acts in which God's kingdom is manifested against Satan and evil spirits, such as the judgment of blindness on the sorcerer, Elymas (Acts 13:9-11).

Each day is filled with excitement and joy untold.
There's no time like the present to watch life unfold
Before my very own eyes; there are miracles never ending.
Will they ever stop, or are they just beginning?

"You asked the question, and I will answer you.
Miracles are unending.
You see, I am God, and you are not.
I know you've heard this before in this exact spot.
It's a good thing to know the simple truth.
Many seem to forget, even from their youth,
How I've protected them and watched over them along the way,
How the angels have been busy each and every day.

Prophecy. To prophesy means to speak for God. The gift of prophecy listed in 1 Corinthians 12:10, as a temporary manifestation of the Spirit, is different from prophecy given as a ministry gift of the church in Ephesians 4:11. Prophecy is given as a ministry gift only to some believers, who then function as prophets within the body of Christ. The Holy Spirit can use every Spirit-filled believer in a spiritual manifestation of prophecy (Acts 2:17-18), when the need arises.

The special gift of prophecy enables a believer to be the vessel used to give a word or revelation from God under the impulse of the Holy Spirit (1 Corinthians 14:24-25, 29-31), and is not a prepared sermon. This gift gives the supernatural ability to proclaim God's present (forth telling) and future truth (foretelling) in such a way that the hearers are moved to respond.

In the Bible, prophecy tells the will of God and challenges believers to live Godly lives (I Corinthians 14:3). It may expose the thoughts in the person's heart, offering comfort, warning, judgment, edification, or exhortation. All prophecies must be tested (1 Corinthians 14:29-32), whether or not they confirm the Word of God (1 John 4:1), if they encourage Godly living, and whether the person delivering the message lives by example (1 Corinthians 12:3).

"It's like there are sometimes
When you have nothing to say;
Then you begin to talk.
Then something comes out
You knew nothing about,
And you begin to wonder,
'Was that lightning or thunder,
Or was that me speaking asunder;
And where did those thoughts come from?
Why now, when it's been years, or maybe never,
When all of a sudden, they sound quite clever?
When I think about things I would never dream,
And it seems like my mind is traveling
Sometimes much faster than I can think or believe,
Even more than I could conceive.
Then I know it can't be me;
It's more than I can receive.'

"It's good to learn to receive
And, even better, when you believe
That there are so many who need to hear
The good news of the gospel that's so great, so dear!"

'It's dear to me, for it's not been so long,
When people would say, "Oh, come on along."
I would go with those I shouldn't be with,
Because I was lonely and needed someone;
Then something would happen.
I would awake from this dream.
It seemed so real, and yet so serene.
I would ask, "Why am I having this dream?"

Then I think back, when the Kings way back when
Would have their dreams and wanted to understand,
What was the meaning? What was God's plan?

'There were prophets back then, who helped them, you see.
They are alive today to help you and me.
When they speak over your life, as it's happened to me,
First check with the Father, if it's to be
His plan, or mine, or others around me.
Some will be plain and simple, you see;
Others may have been confirmation to me;
Then there are others so far out, it seems,
They look impossible in the natural this day.

'All things are possible with God, when you say,
"I believe and receive it. I'll trust and obey."'

Discerning of spirits. This gift gives the supernatural ability to determine, with assurance, whether a certain action has its source in God, man, or Satan. In the last days, discernment of spirits is crucial, because of false teachers. This does not mean we can go around announcing what spirit is in each person.

Kinds of tongues. Tongues as a supernatural manifestation may be an existing language or one that is unintelligible and hasn't been learned. The words are unknown, even to the one who speaks them. Our spirit makes way for the Holy Spirit, building up and edifying our spirit (1 Corinthians 14:2, 4, 15, 28; Jude 20). This edification takes place without our ever knowing what is said. Such edification is experienced individually by praying in tongues.   We are also encouraged to sing in the spirit (1 Corinthians 14:15).

The inspiration of speaking in tongues in a group will be accompanied by the interpretation of what is spoken, often from someone across the room, sometimes by someone not acquainted with the first believer. These messages give revelation, knowledge, prophecy, or teaching directed toward the entire body of believers, who can then participate in this Spirit-inspired message, edifying the whole body   (1 Corinthians 14:3, 6, 13, 27-28).

Interpretation of tongues. The Holy Spirit gives the ability to understand and speak the meaning of a message given in tongues, and the interpretation may be given to the one who first speaks in tongues or to someone else. If we speak in tongues, we should pray for the gift of interpretation (1 Corinthians 14:13).

"Go this day, as you must remember,
That My plans for you are not getting dimmer,
But brighter and brighter, as each day comes forth;
For what is happening this hour
Is showing you how awesome My power

Can be to set My people free!

"Go this day, My son and daughter,
To know and believe that you are much smarter
Because of Me,
And walk with confidence to receive
All that you truly believe
Is yours, because of Me,
As I am your Heavenly Father;
For you are My son and daughter.
Be filled with My joy this very hour
And continue to absorb and devour,
Until it becomes a part of your soul;
And then you will know that you know.

"How can I speak with such power this hour?

"For I know you are ready to receive My plans,
As they unfold to benefit man;
As he is ready to take a stand in this land,
To band together, and walk hand-in-hand.
This is the unity, which must prevail
For My people to survive in this dying world;
For the day is coming, and soon it shall be,
When those who are ready shall all be set free.

"Go this day, and tell those you see
That Jesus is coming. He's coming for thee!
The time is now! There's no time to delay!
It could very well happen this very day!
Be watchful and ready each day as you pray,
And know I'll never leave you this day or the next.
You've read it and read it. It's all in the text;

"So read it some more, until there's a door
To walk through, and then you will know,
As you journey with Me,
That My people who seek Me
Shall all become free."

"Many of My people are so busy going here and there trying to find their own place or niche in life, taking time and spending quality time alone with Me, yet not being able to understand why they are feeling such frustration and panic, with no evidence of peace and tranquility within their very own soul.

"Others are choosing to believe a lie about who I am, and who they are, so busy with being busy (<u>b</u>ound <u>u</u>nder <u>S</u>atan's <u>y</u>oke) for the sake of the Gospel, creating such a bad image about what a Christian is supposed to be all about; when in truth, those who profess not to be a Christian know more about how a real Christian should live than those who say they are one.

"Go forth in this very day and hour to examine your own life and actions, asking yourself, 'Who do others say that I am? What do they see in my life? Is Jesus glorified and exalted in my life in everything I think, say, or do?'"

ABOUT THE AUTHORS:

Don H. Duke, the youngest of four children, was born in Lamesa, Texas, in the corner of the Lamesa Cemetery in 1941. His father kept all the burial records for Dawson County, and the family lived in a home inside the perimeter of the cemetery. As a youth, he worked with his father and brothers farming adjacent property and helping his father care for the cemetery.

Don served four years in the United States Air Force Security Service in Communications, and was stationed in Japan during the Viet Nam War. He received a degree in Business Administration from Sul Ross State University in Alpine, Texas.

Sharon, born in Oklahoma, and Don were married in 1972 and raised four children, Kevin, Mindy, Jason, and Amber Lee. Sharon worked in the furniture industry until the year 2000 and now serves with her husband in the ministry.

Don spent thirty-five years in the furniture industry in Texas, Missouri, Colorado, New Mexico, and Oklahoma. One night, around 3:30 A.M. in August, 1993, Don woke from a deep sleep, hearing these words in his spirit, "Set My people free."

The family moved to Tulsa in 1995. Don and Sharon attended The Checotah Revival in February, 2000. They founded Rainbow Jubilee Ministry in April and ended their careers in August, 2000, giving away everything, keeping only what they could carry in their car.

After volunteering at inner-city ministries in Dallas and Los Angeles, their journey took them to Alaska, Canada, Israel, and most of the central and western states, as witnesses, ministering in food chapels, nursing homes, churches, prisons, and missions.